The Witch of the Elements

Working with the Four Elements for Balance and Harmony

The Witch of the Elements: Working with the Four Elements for Balance and Harmony

Contents

Chapter 1: Introduction to Elemental Witchcraft

In every gust of wind, in the raging inferno of a wildfire, in the tranquil lapping of waves against the shore, and in the resilience of the towering mountains, we bear witness to the extraordinary dance of the elements. Earth, Air, Fire, and Water—these are more than just classifications of the natural world; they are the cornerstones of life and the foundational forces in the practice of elemental witchcraft.

Elemental witchcraft, as the name implies, is a magical path that focuses on the energy of the four classical elements. It is a practice that speaks to our deepest connection to the natural world and taps into the vibrations and inherent powers that each element possesses. As we delve into this age-old practice, we embark on a journey of balance, harmony, and transformation. This exploration helps us to understand not just the world around us, but also the world within us, and it allows us to manipulate energies for manifesting our desires, achieving spiritual growth, and maintaining equilibrium in our lives.

Let's begin by introducing the four elements.

Earth: The first of the elements, Earth is the embodiment of stability, resilience, and abundance. It is the element that grounds us, offering a base from which we can grow and thrive. In witchcraft, Earth symbolizes not only the physical plane, but also the framework of our lives: our health, our home, our resources, and our senses. It represents fertility, nurturing, and growth. When we invoke Earth energy in our magical workings, we tap into the foundational strength that enables us to manifest our desires into physical reality.

Air: The second element, Air, is linked to the mind, intellect, and communication. It represents our thoughts, ideas, hopes, and dreams. It symbolizes change and movement, carrying away the old and bringing in the new, much like the winds that sweep across our planet. Working with Air in witchcraft, we harness the power of our minds to seek clarity, improve communication, and cultivate inspiration.

Fire: The third element, Fire, is the embodiment of transformation, passion, and willpower. It is both a creator and a destroyer, capable of sparking life or reducing everything to ashes. In witchcraft, Fire stands for courage, motivation, desire, and transformation. When we call upon the energy of Fire, we tap into its transformative power to incinerate our fears, ignite our passions, and propel us toward our goals.

Water: The final element, Water, symbolizes emotions, intuition, and healing. It represents our feelings, our intuition, and our deeper psychic selves. Water can be calm and healing, like a tranquil lake, or it can be turbulent and overwhelming, like a raging sea. By invoking Water in our magical practice, we navigate our emotional landscapes, enhance our intuitive abilities, and facilitate healing.

By understanding these elements and their metaphysical properties, we begin to see how they interact and influence the world around us and within us. They are not separate, but interconnected, each one affecting and balancing the others. The elements exist in a state of constant interaction, shaping the world, the seasons, and even our bodies.

For instance, consider our physical selves. Our bodies are a living testament to the interplay of the elements. Earth forms our flesh and bones, Fire fuels our metabolism and vital heat, Air fills our lungs and aids our speech, and Water flows through our blood and regulates our bodily functions. The harmony of these elements within us determines our health and vitality.

In the external world, we see this balance reflected in the changing seasons: Earth in the fertility and growth of spring, Air in the warmth and clarity of summer, Fire in the transformation and shedding of autumn, and Water in the introspection and tranquility of winter.

Elemental witchcraft allows us to tap into these elemental forces and use them in our magical workings. But it's not just about wielding power—it's about understanding the delicate balance of nature, both within and around us, and learning to align with that balance. It's about fostering a deeper connection with the natural world and recognizing our role in the grand tapestry of existence.

Through the chapters that follow, we will delve deeper into each element, exploring their properties, correspondences, and how to incorporate them into our practice. We will discuss rituals and meditations that will help you connect with each element and harness their energies. This journey is not about mastering nature; it's about becoming one with it. It's about understanding the rhythm of the elements, dancing to their beat, and letting their energy flow through you.

As we walk this path together, may you find balance, may you find harmony, and above all, may you find yourself within the dance of the elements.

Chapter 2: Understanding the Witch within

In the pursuit of harmony and balance through elemental witchcraft, one key factor is often overlooked by many: the witch themselves. Before you can truly connect with the elements and use them to bring about desired changes, you need to understand yourself. This chapter is a self-exploration exercise, placing emphasis on introspection and self-awareness as a cornerstone for successful practice in witchcraft.

Think of yourself as the fifth element, the ether or spirit. You are the medium through which the four elements—Earth, Air, Fire, and Water—are manipulated and directed. If you are out of balance, it is likely that your interaction with the elements will be less effective, or even chaotic. So, before we venture into the mysteries of the elements, let's first embark on the most profound journey of all—the journey inward.

Self-awareness is an ongoing process. It is not something that you can achieve in a day or a week. It requires dedication, patience, and most importantly, honesty. Honesty, in this context, refers to acknowledging your strengths and weaknesses, your desires and fears, your achievements and failures. It is about looking at yourself in the mirror of truth, without bias or judgment.

Meditation can be an effective tool for enhancing self-awareness. You don't have to meditate for hours on end; even a few minutes each day can have profound effects. Begin with a simple mindfulness practice. Sit in a quiet place, close your eyes, and focus on your breath. When your mind wanders (and it will), gently bring it back to the breath. The key here is not to stop the thoughts, but to observe them without engagement. This practice helps create a gap between you, the observer, and your thoughts, enabling you to understand your mental patterns better.

A more advanced form of meditation is self-inquiry, a practice rooted in ancient spiritual traditions. The goal of self-inquiry is to understand the nature of the self, to ask the question, "Who am I?" You start by discarding what you are not. You are not your body, as it changes with time. You are not your mind, as your thoughts and emotions are constantly in flux. You are not your roles, titles, or societal identities, as they are external constructs. So, who are you? This practice can be deeply transformative, leading to the realization of your true, unchanging nature.

Now, let's talk about the witch's shadow. The concept of the shadow self was first proposed by Carl Jung, the famous Swiss psychiatrist. According to Jung, the shadow is the part of the psyche that contains all the aspects of ourselves that we deny or reject—our fears, insecurities, negative patterns, and destructive behaviors. In the context of witchcraft, the shadow represents the inner self that needs to be accepted and integrated for a balanced practice.

Working with the shadow is not easy. It involves facing your deepest fears and darkest parts. However, it is an essential part of your journey as a witch. The first step in shadow work is acknowledging the existence of the shadow. You can't change what you don't recognize. Next, engage with your shadow through meditation, journaling, or dream work. Ask your shadow what it wants you to know. What fears or traumas are it holding onto? How are these affecting your life and your craft?

Acceptance is the next step. Accept that these shadow aspects are part of you, but they don't define you. Forgive yourself for any mistakes or failures, and show compassion to your shadow. Finally, integrate your shadow. This doesn't mean that you let your negative patterns control you. Instead, it means understanding that every aspect of yourself has a role to play, and using this understanding to grow and evolve.

Remember, a witch is not someone who denies the darkness within, but someone who understands it, accepts it, and learns from it. As you grow in self-awareness and integrate your shadow, your practice with the elements will become more effective and balanced. You will not just be a witch who works with the elements, but a witch who is in harmony with the elements— both outside and within.

Chapter 3: The Earth Element - Grounding and Stability

As we begin our exploration of the Earth element, we delve into a realm rich in stability, nurture, and the whispers of ancient wisdom. Associated with the North, Earth represents the solid ground beneath our feet, the unyielding mountains, and the abundant forests, filling our world with life and providing us a platform upon which to live and grow. Earth is the most tangible of the elements, the one we can touch, feel, and connect with the most directly. It symbolizes physicality, prosperity, and grounding.

The Symbolism of Earth

Earth, in its essence, is the manifestation of stability and permanence. It resonates with energies of steadfastness, reliability, and patience. Symbolically, Earth represents the body, physical health, prosperity, and grounding. It is the backbone that supports all life, providing the nutrients necessary for growth. Its strength lies in its quiet solidity, a resilience that spans time and endures even the harshest conditions.

When you think of Earth, visualize a mighty tree, its roots digging deep into the soil, anchoring it firmly in place, while its branches reach out to touch the sky. This is the balance that Earth brings to our lives, grounding us yet allowing us to grow.

Correspondences of Earth

In elemental magic, each element has specific correspondences that are aligned with its energies. Here are the primary correspondences of the Earth element:

Direction: North

Colors: Green, brown, black

Season: Winter

Time of day: Midnight

Senses: Touch

Zodiac Signs: Taurus, Virgo, Capricorn

Tarot Suit: Pentacles

Magical Tools: Pentacle, salt, stones

Herbs: Patchouli, Vetiver, Magnolia

Understanding these correspondences helps to focus your intention and channel the Earth element's energy effectively in your rituals and meditations.

The Role of Earth in Witchcraft

In witchcraft, Earth serves as the grounding force that balances the energies of the other elements. Without Earth, our thoughts (Air), passion (Fire), and emotions (Water) would have no container.

Earth is often invoked for rituals involving prosperity, abundance, stability, grounding, and fertility. It provides the fertile ground where our magical intentions can take root and blossom. Its energy nurtures our physical bodies, healing us and keeping us healthy.

Ritual for Grounding

Grounding is a practice of balancing your energy by reconnecting with the Earth. When we're ungrounded, we might feel dizzy, disconnected, or easily influenced by external forces. Here's a simple grounding ritual you can perform:

Materials: A green or brown candle, a small bowl of soil, and a piece of clear quartz

Sit comfortably and light the candle in front of you.

Place the bowl of soil before the candle and hold the clear quartz in your hands.

Close your eyes and visualize a beam of light descending from the sky, entering through the top of your head, and flowing through your body.

Imagine this light flowing through your feet and into the ground, like roots burrowing deep into the Earth.

As you breathe, visualize the Earth's energy moving up these roots, filling your body with grounding, stable energy. Feel this energy pulsing within you, anchoring you firmly to the Earth.

Open your eyes, extinguish the candle, and thank the Earth for her grounding energy.

Meditation for Stability

Meditation is a potent tool for connecting with the elements, and Earth-focused meditation can bring about stability and peace.

Find a quiet, comfortable spot, preferably outdoors where you can touch the soil or sit under a tree. Close your eyes and imagine yourself as a tree. Feel your roots extending deep into the Earth, and your branches reaching for the sky. As you breathe in, visualize the Earth's nurturing energy flowing up your roots and into your body. As you breathe out, imagine any stress or tension being released down into the Earth. Continue this visualization for as long as you wish, then open your eyes and thank the Earth for her stability.

Ritual for Material Manifestation

As Earth represents prosperity and material wealth, you can invoke this element to manifest your material desires.

Materials: Five coins, a green candle, a piece of paper and a pen

Light the green candle and place the five coins around it, forming a pentacle.

On the piece of paper, write down your specific material desire, be it a new job, financial stability, or a new home.

Fold the paper and place it in the middle of the coin pentacle.

Visualize your desire coming to fruition. See yourself receiving the abundance you seek, and feel the joy it brings.

Thank the Earth for her abundant gifts, then leave the setup undisturbed until the candle burns out on its own.

Remember, magic is not a shortcut or a way to bypass effort. These rituals are meant to supplement your practical efforts, aligning your energies to your intentions, and helping you manifest your desires more effectively.

The Earth element invites us to celebrate the physical world, to embrace the beauty of nature, and to ground ourselves in the present moment. Working with Earth can bring stability, nurture our bodies, and help manifest our material needs. It teaches us the value of patience and the joy of steady growth. As you deepen your connection with Earth, may you find yourself more grounded, more stable, and more in tune with the rhythms of life.

Chapter 4: Working with Earth - Rituals and Practices

In the previous chapter, we delved into the realm of Earth, learning about its grounding and nurturing properties, and how this element's energy influences our physical existence, prosperity, and stability. Now, it's time to walk on the practical path, to put our understanding into practice by involving ourselves in rituals and meditations that harness the Earth's energy. Here, we will delve into rituals for grounding, prosperity, and protection, and meditations to deepen our connection with the Earth.

Ritual 1: Grounding with Earth

This ritual will help you ground your energy, making you feel more stable and connected to your physical surroundings. For this ritual, you will need:

A small bowl of soil or a potted plant

A piece of clear quartz crystal

A green candle

Steps:

Begin by finding a quiet place where you won't be disturbed. This could be indoors or outdoors, but somewhere you feel comfortable and connected to the Earth.

Light the green candle, representing the Earth element, and place the bowl of soil or the potted plant before you.

Hold the clear quartz crystal in your hands and close your eyes. Visualize a white light enveloping you, protecting you from external energies.

Deeply inhale and exhale, visualizing the energy from the Earth flowing up from your feet, grounding and stabilizing you. Feel the solidness of the Earth beneath you.

Place the crystal on the soil or the plant, saying, "I ground myself in the nurturing energy of the Earth. I am stable, I am secure, I am connected."

Leave the crystal on the soil and let the candle burn out safely. Keep the crystal as a talisman of grounding.

Ritual 2: Prosperity Ritual

This ritual invites the prosperous energy of the Earth into your life. For this ritual, you will need:

Five green candles

A coin

A piece of paper and pen

Steps:

Begin by setting up a quiet space where you will not be disturbed. Arrange the five green candles in a pentagram pattern, symbolizing the Earth element and its connection to prosperity.

In the center of the pentagram, place the coin, representing material wealth.

On the piece of paper, write down what prosperity means to you. This could be financial stability, a new job, a home, etc.

Light the candles, starting from the top and moving clockwise. As you light each one, say, "I call upon the abundant energy of the Earth."

Hold the piece of paper over the coin and say, "Earth, nurture my intentions as you nurture the seeds in the ground. As the seeds grow into plants, so too may my prosperity grow."

Leave the paper and coin within the circle of candles until they burn down. Bury the coin in a plant or garden as an offering to Earth and keep the paper as a reminder of your intention.

Ritual 3: Protection Ritual

Earth's energy is not only nurturing but also protective. For this ritual, you will need:

Four black tourmaline stones

A brown candle

Steps:

In a quiet space, place the brown candle in the center of your space, symbolizing the Earth.

Place the four black tourmaline stones around the candle, forming a square. These stones will serve as your protective boundaries.

Light the candle, saying, "I call upon the energy of the Earth. May these stones ground me and protect me."

Visualize a brown light emanating from the candle, reaching out to the stones and forming a protective barrier around you.

When you are ready, extinguish the candle. Leave the stones in place as long as you feel the need for protection.

Meditation: Connecting with the Earth

Meditation can be a powerful way to connect with the Earth element. Find a quiet space, ideally outside where you can touch the Earth.

Sit or stand barefoot on the ground, closing your eyes and taking deep breaths.

Visualize roots growing from your feet and going deep into the Earth.

As you inhale, visualize the energy of the Earth moving up through these roots and spreading through your body. As you exhale, visualize any negative energy being released back into the Earth to be transformed.

Continue this cycle of breath and visualization for as long as you need.

Remember, the key to any ritual or meditation is intention. As you work with the Earth element, keep your intentions clear and focused. You are not commanding the Earth, but rather working with it, acknowledging its energy and influence in your life. Practice these rituals and meditations regularly, and you will develop a deep, resonating connection with the Earth.

Chapter 5: The Air Element - Intellect and Communication

Air is one of the four cardinal elements, traditionally considered the bridge between the physical and the spiritual realms. It is an element of movement, of new beginnings, of knowledge, and of connection. In witchcraft, it is commonly associated with the intellectual and communicative aspects of life. This chapter explores the characteristics, powers, and significance of the Air element, and how to effectively harness its energy to enhance intellect, communication, and creative expression.

Air has always been an element of mystery and magic. Invisible to the human eye, yet immensely powerful, it surrounds us everywhere we go, filling our lungs and bringing life into our bodies with each breath we take. Air carries our words when we speak, our thoughts when we ponder, and our dreams when we sleep. It is ever-present, ever-changing, and ever-mysterious, making it an integral part of our lives and our magical practices.

The Air element corresponds to the East, the direction of the rising sun, of new beginnings, and of wisdom. Its time is dawn, that magical hour when the world is waking up, filled with potential and the promise of a new day. Its season is spring, a time of rebirth and renewal, when the world shakes off the cold of winter and bursts into vibrant life. This connection with the East, dawn, and spring gives the Air element a potent energy of intellect, creativity, and rebirth.

In the realm of the senses, Air is associated with hearing, the sense that connects us with the world around us and allows us to communicate with others. Through sound, carried by the wind, we can understand and be understood, we can express our thoughts, our feelings, and our desires. This strong link with communication makes Air magic particularly useful for any work involving knowledge, understanding, teaching, and learning.

Air is also linked with the power of the mind, the realm of intellect. It rules over our thoughts, our ideas, our creativity, and our imagination. It's the element of scholars, writers, poets, and artists, of those who thrive on ideas and creative expression. When you need clarity of thought, when you need inspiration, when you need to learn or teach, turn to Air.

So how can you connect with this powerful element and incorporate it into your witchcraft practice?

Firstly, become aware of the Air around you. Notice its touch on your skin, its sound in your ears, its taste in your mouth. Recognize its presence in every breath you take. Watch the leaves rustle in the wind, watch the clouds float across the sky. Listen to the birds singing, to the rustle of the wind. Breathe, and with each breath, visualize the Air energy entering your body, filling you with its clarity, its wisdom, its inspiration.

Meditation is a powerful tool to connect with the Air element. You can do a simple meditation where you sit comfortably, close your eyes, and focus on your breath. Feel the Air entering your body, filling your lungs, and then leaving your body, carrying away with it any negative energy, any doubts, any fears. Visualize yourself surrounded by a gentle breeze, carrying whispers of wisdom and creativity to your ears.

Air is often represented in magical practice by tools such as the wand or the athame, symbols of direction, will, and action. You can use these tools to draw Air symbols or sigils in the air during your rituals, to call on the powers of the Air element.

Air magic is also particularly suited for spellwork involving communication, travel, and intellectual pursuits. Whether you're seeking inspiration for a creative project, looking for clarity in decision-making, or trying to improve your communication skills, Air magic can be of great help. You can use incense, feathers, or wind chimes in your rituals, anything that connects you with the energy of Air.

The Air element is also connected with certain deities, such as the Greek god Hermes, the Egyptian god Thoth, and the Norse god Odin, all gods of knowledge, wisdom, and communication.

You can call on these deities in your Air magic rituals, ask for their guidance, their wisdom, their inspiration.

Working with the Air element requires open-mindedness and flexibility. Like the wind that blows freely, changing direction at will, Air magic is about embracing change, about being open to new ideas, new experiences, new beginnings. It's about communicating your truth, about expressing your creativity, about following your intellect and your intuition.

Remember, though, that like all elements, Air has a dual nature. It can be a gentle breeze, bringing refreshment and inspiration, but it can also be a storm, bringing chaos and confusion.

Balance in all things is key. Use Air magic wisely, respect its power, and it can bring great wisdom, clarity, and creativity into your life.

The Air element is an essential part of witchcraft, representing intellect, communication, and creative expression.

Connecting with this element, understanding its characteristics and powers, can greatly enhance your magical practice, opening your mind, awakening your creativity, and improving your communication skills.

So breathe, listen, and let the whispers of the wind guide your path.

Chapter 6: Working with Air - Rituals and Practices

Air is the element of communication, ideas, and intellect. It represents inspiration, knowledge, and change. Working with the element of air is about bringing in more of these qualities into our lives. In this chapter, we will guide you through practical applications of Air magic, including rituals for improving communication, enhancing creativity, and boosting intellect, alongside meditations to deepen your connection with the Air element.

Ritual for Improving Communication

The first ritual we'll discuss is aimed at improving communication. It's particularly beneficial when you're preparing for important conversations, presentations, or when you wish to clear misunderstandings with someone. You'll need the following items:

A feather (any type)

Blue or white candles

Incense (sage, lavender, or mint)

A piece of paper and pen

Begin by setting up your space. Light the candles and incense, and place the feather in front of you. Ensure you won't be disturbed during the ritual.

Write down on the paper the specifics of the communication issue you're experiencing. Be honest and specific.

Hold the feather in your dominant hand and visualize the element of air surrounding you. Feel its gentle, swirling energy.

As you inhale the scent of the incense, read out what you've written, then say, "Element of Air, lend me your clarity and ease, let my words flow freely and reach where they must. So mote it be."

Leave the feather on the paper, blow out the candle, and leave the room, trusting that the Air element will carry your intentions forward.

Ritual for Enhancing Creativity

The next ritual is designed to enhance your creativity. This can be beneficial for artists, writers, or anyone involved in creative work. You'll need the following items:

A yellow candle

Incense (preferably citrus-based like lemon or bergamot)

A small piece of clear quartz

A piece of paper and a pen

Begin by setting up your space, lighting the candle and the incense. Hold the quartz in your hand and sit comfortably.

On the paper, write down areas where you seek creative inspiration or where you feel blocked.

Hold the piece of quartz in your hand and visualize the air around you vibrating with creative energy.

Say the following or similar: "Element of Air, spark my mind, let inspiration flow like the wind, let creativity emerge freely. So mote it be."

Keep the quartz near your workspace or carry it with you as a reminder of your intention.

Ritual for Boosting Intellect

Our final ritual focuses on boosting intellect, helpful for students or anyone seeking to learn something new. You'll need:

An incense stick (sage, rosemary, or peppermint)

A blue or yellow candle

A clear quartz or a fluorite stone

A book or any item representing your studies

Set up your sacred space, light the candle and the incense. Place the stone and the item representing your studies before you.

Take a moment to focus on the item representing your studies, thinking about the knowledge you wish to acquire.

Hold the stone, visualize the air around you glowing with the energy of intellect and wisdom.

Speak your intention: "Element of Air, heighten my intellect, grant me the wisdom to comprehend, to learn, and to grow. So mote it be."

Keep the stone with you when studying as a tangible reminder of your intention.

Meditations for Connecting with Air

Connecting with the Air element through meditation can deepen your understanding and relationship with this element. Here are two meditations you can practice.

Breath Awareness Meditation

Find a quiet place where you can sit undisturbed. Close your eyes and start focusing on your breath.

Imagine the breath as a tangible form of the air element, coming in and out of your body, carrying energy and life.

As you breathe in, imagine the air bringing clarity, creativity, and wisdom. As you breathe out, imagine releasing confusion and stagnant energy.

Practice this for at least 5-10 minutes each day to feel a deeper connection with the air element.

Outdoor Air Meditation

Find a safe outdoor spot where you can feel the breeze, such as a park or your backyard.

Close your eyes and focus on the sensations of the air on your skin. Feel its touch, its temperature.

Listen to the sounds carried by the wind—the rustling leaves, the distant noises.

As you breathe, visualize the air element's qualities infusing with your being.

The rituals and practices of Air magic provide a path to harnessing the element's power, enhancing our communication, creativity, and intellect. By deepening our connection to this lively and dynamic element, we can evoke a profound transformation in our lives. The journey with the Air element is one of self-discovery, growth, and continuous learning. In the next chapter, we will explore the element of Fire, the element of transformation, passion, and willpower.

Chapter 7: The Fire Element - Transformation and Willpower

Among the four elements, Fire is considered the most transformative. It's associated with energy, passion, willpower, and change. It symbolizes not only the literal flames, but also the metaphysical energies that motivate, drive, and catalyze. In witchcraft, Fire holds a unique place due to its dynamic, transformative qualities. Fire is both a creator and a destroyer, a symbol of rebirth and change.

The Fire element is associated with the South direction in many witchcraft traditions. In astrology, Fire corresponds to the signs of Aries, Leo, and Sagittarius, known for their charismatic, adventurous, and passionate characteristics. It's linked with the suit of wands in the tarot, representing action, inspiration, and initiative.

Fire is not only outside of us, represented by the sun, a candle flame, or a crackling bonfire; it's also within us. It represents our life-force, our spirit, our will, our ambition, and our passions. When we talk about someone being "on fire," we're referring to that individual's passion, motivation, and energetic charge – all attributes of the Fire element.

Fire has been revered throughout history and across cultures. It's seen as a primal force, essential for survival, yet potentially dangerous if not handled respectfully. From ancient rituals around hearths and bonfires to the eternal flames kept in temples and sacred places, Fire is a physical reminder of transformation, passion, and the life force itself. Harnessing the power of Fire means inviting change, passion, and motivation into our lives.

In witchcraft, Fire is employed in numerous ways. Witches may use candles, bonfires, or symbolic flames during their rituals and spellcasting. Fire can be used to burn objects, symbolizing the release of old energies and the welcoming of new ones. It can also serve as a conduit for messages to the spiritual realm, as seen in the practice of burning written intentions or messages to ancestors.

Working with Fire should be approached with respect and caution. Its destructive power is as potent as its creative force. As with all elemental forces, the aim is not to control but to work in harmony, understanding, and respecting Fire's nature.

When you invite the energy of Fire into your life, you're welcoming transformation and change. It's the element of rebirth, a signal that you're ready to burn away the old to make way for the new. In this sense, Fire becomes a powerful ally in spells for change, new beginnings, and releasing the past.

Fire also fuels our willpower. It gives us the energy to pursue our goals, to assert our will, to stand up and take action. In this sense, it's an excellent element to work with when you're seeking courage or motivation.

But Fire isn't only about change and action; it's also associated with passion. This includes not only romantic passion but passion in all forms – for life, for interests, for causes. Fire stirs the heart and soul, inspiring us, driving us forward, illuminating the path with its bright flame.

To tap into the power of Fire, you might start by spending time each day with the element. This could be as simple as lighting a candle and focusing on the flame. Feel the heat, watch the dancing light, and connect with the transformative power it represents.

Meditation is another powerful tool. Visualize yourself bathed in a warm, orange-red light. Feel the heat penetrating your skin, fueling your inner fire, stoking your willpower, burning away anything that no longer serves you.

When working with Fire, it's crucial to keep balance in mind. Fire's power can easily tip from motivational to consuming, from passionate to obsessive. Invoking Fire involves both respecting its power and understanding its potential for imbalance. It's important to balance Fire with the other elements, grounding with Earth, seeking emotional balance with Water, and clarity with Air.

By understanding and working with the Fire element, we can harness its transformative power to instigate change, bolster our willpower, and fuel our passions. With respect and balance, we can incorporate Fire into our witchcraft practices, using it as a powerful tool for personal growth and transformation. Fire teaches us that from the ashes, new life can emerge, and change, though sometimes challenging, is an essential part of life's cycle.

Chapter 8: Working with Fire - Rituals and Practices

Fire has always held a unique place in human consciousness. It's not just a symbol of warmth, light, and safety; it represents passion, will, and transformation. In this chapter, we'll dive into some specific ways you can harness this energy for courage, transformation, and love.

To start, let's remember that Fire can be both creator and destroyer. Just as a forest fire clears the way for new growth, so too can Fire help you burn away what's no longer serving you, to make room for the new.

Ritual for Courage

The first ritual we'll discuss uses Fire to ignite your inner strength and bravery. Remember, courage isn't about not being afraid—it's about facing fear and acting despite it.

You'll need:

A red or orange candle (symbolizing courage and bravery)

A piece of paper and a pen

A fire-safe bowl

Begin by finding a quiet space where you won't be disturbed. Ground and center yourself. Visualize yourself drawing energy up from the earth and down from the sky, meeting in your heart center, swirling in a vortex of pure energy.

On the piece of paper, write down what you're afraid of, what's holding you back. Be honest and specific.

Next, light the candle and focus on the flame. Feel its heat, watch its dance. Imagine this flame as your courage, small but mighty.

Now, take the paper in your hand and say the following (or similar) words aloud:

"I acknowledge my fears, but I will not let them control me. With this flame, I ignite my courage. As this paper turns to ash, so too does my fear."

Carefully set the paper on fire using the candle's flame and place it in the fire-safe bowl. As the paper burns, imagine your fear being consumed by the flame, transforming into a powerful, courageous energy.

As you watch the last embers die, visualize the courage imbuing your entire being. Take as much time as you need. When you're ready, gently blow out the candle, thanking the element of Fire for its help.

Ritual for Transformation

Fire is a powerful catalyst for change. This ritual helps you tap into that transformative energy, allowing you to shed what no longer serves you and embrace new beginnings.

You'll need:

A black candle (symbolizing release and transformation)

A piece of paper and a pen

A fire-safe bowl

Like before, find a quiet space and ground yourself. Light the black candle, letting its flame symbolize the transformative energy of Fire.

On the paper, write down the aspects of your life that you wish to change or let go of.

Hold the paper up to the flame and say, "With Fire, I release what no longer serves me. From the ashes, a stronger, better me shall arise."

Burn the paper in the fire-safe bowl, letting the flame consume your written words. As the fire reduces your words to ashes, visualize those aspects of your life you wished to release being transformed, leaving space for new growth.

When you're ready, extinguish the candle, offering thanks to the element of Fire.

Ritual for Love

This final ritual invites love into your life. Whether it's self-love or romantic love, the Fire element can help spark these emotions.

You'll need:

A pink or red candle (representing love)

Rose quartz or any love-associated crystal

A piece of paper and a pen

A fire-safe bowl

As always, begin by grounding and centering yourself. Light the candle, and place the rose quartz near the flame. On the paper, write down what love means to you, or the kind of love you want to attract.

Hold the paper over the flame and say, "I kindle this flame in the name of Love. As this paper burns, may it draw to me the love I seek."

Carefully burn the paper, letting the flame consume your written words. Visualize the flame's warmth radiating out and drawing love into your life.

When you're ready, extinguish the candle, holding onto the warmth of the flame in your heart.

Meditation for Connection with Fire

This meditation helps deepen your connection with the Fire element.

Find a quiet space where you won't be disturbed. Sit comfortably, close your eyes, and take a few deep breaths.

Visualize a flame in your heart center. With every inhale, see this flame grow a little bigger, feel it become a little warmer. With every exhale, imagine this warmth spreading through your entire body.

Stay with this visualization for a while. Feel the strength and energy of the fire within you. Feel the courage, transformation, and love it brings.

When you're ready, visualize the flame shrinking back down, settling in your heart. Take a few more deep breaths, then gently open your eyes.

Practicing these rituals and meditation allows you to form a deeper bond with the Fire element. Remember always to work respectfully and responsibly with Fire, understanding its potent and transformative power. Embrace its energy and let it embolden your witchcraft practice. Remember, like a flame, you are powerful, fierce, and ever-changing.

Chapter 9: The Water Element - Emotions and Intuition

Water, the element of emotion, intuition, compassion, and mystery, has a significant place in witchcraft. This chapter aims to deepen your understanding of the water element, exploring its myriad forms and its role in the magical arts. Known as the symbol of the subconscious, water is the gateway to understanding our feelings, accessing our intuition, and developing our psychic abilities.

The Elemental Signature of Water

Water is fluid, adaptive, and profound. Like its physical form, it represents adaptability and transformation. Yet, it also stands for depth, as it holds the mysteries of the deep ocean. In the realm of witchcraft, water is tied to our emotional landscape. It represents our feelings and our ability to empathize with others.

Water is also closely linked with our intuitive faculties. It symbolizes our inner voice, our gut feeling, the part of us that knows something without logical explanation. Many witches believe that water can enhance our intuitive abilities, helping us delve into the depths of our subconscious.

The Symbolism of Water

In ancient cultures, water has always been considered a powerful symbol. The Greeks associated water with Aphrodite, the goddess of love, embodying its association with emotion. In Celtic mythology, water was seen as a gateway to the Otherworld, reflecting its ties to intuition and the subconscious. Water is the womb from which all life originates, linking it to birth, fertility, and creation.

The Moon's gravitational pull impacts the tides, making water also symbolic of cycles, ebbs and flows, and the passage of time. Its mercurial nature mirrors our emotions, which can shift and change like the tide.

Working with the Water Element in Witchcraft

Using water in your witchcraft practice can deepen your emotional understanding and enhance your intuition. Here are some ways you can work with this element:

Water Meditation: Meditating near a body of water can help you connect with its energy. If you can't physically go to a water source, you can use a bowl of water or even visualize a body of water in your mind's eye. Try to sync your breathing with the rhythm of the waves or the flow of the stream.

Ritual Bathing: Ritual baths are a potent way to harness water's energy. You can add herbs, essential oils, or salts related to your intent. A ritual bath can serve to cleanse negative energy, promote self-love, or enhance intuition.

Water Scrying: This ancient form of divination involves gazing into a water surface to receive messages or insights. This practice can help enhance your intuition and tap into your subconscious mind.

Potion Making: Brewing teas or infusions can also be a form of water magic. The intent you imbue into the water as you craft your potion amplifies the effect.

Rituals and Practices for Emotion and Intuition

Connecting with water involves understanding your emotions and enhancing your intuition. Here are some specific practices that might help:

Emotional Healing Ritual: For this ritual, you'll need a bowl of water and a handful of sea salt. Write down any emotional pain or trauma you want to release on a piece of paper. Dissolve the sea salt in the water, visualizing it purifying and cleansing the water. Burn the paper over the bowl, letting the ashes fall into the water. Imagine your emotional pain being absorbed by the water. Dispose of the water outdoors, returning it to nature, and envision your emotional pain being washed away.

Intuition Enhancing Meditation: Find a quiet space near a body of water or use a bowl of water. Light a blue or white candle (associated with water and intuition) and sit comfortably. Gaze into the water, allowing your mind to become still. As your thoughts subside, pay attention to any images, feelings, or thoughts that arise. This practice can help you tune into your intuition and psychic abilities.

Water, with its soothing and healing properties, plays a crucial role in the life of a witch. It teaches us to be adaptable, helps us connect with our emotions, and deepens our intuition. By working with water, we learn to flow with life's currents, understand our emotional depth, and tap into the wisdom of our subconscious. And so, we become one with the element, navigating life with enhanced emotional intelligence and intuitive guidance.

Chapter 10: Working with Water - Rituals and Practices

Water, the element most closely linked to our emotional state, intuition, and the realm of love and friendship, is the focus of our tenth chapter. Just as a river's current shapes the land, water shapes our internal landscape. It nurtures, cleanses, heals, and provides deep emotional understanding. In this chapter, we will explore practical ways of harnessing this versatile and deeply transformative element through rituals and meditations.

Ritual for Emotional Healing

This ritual can be performed when you are experiencing overwhelming emotions and are in need of emotional clarity and healing.

Materials Needed:

A bowl of spring or rainwater

A piece of blue agate or moonstone

Lavender or chamomile essential oil

White candle

Paper and pen

Steps:

Start by creating a sacred space. Light the white candle and place it on your altar or work area. The candle flame represents the element of Fire, which will work in harmony with the Water element to purify and transform.

Take a few moments to ground and center yourself. Feel the Earth beneath you and the sky above you. Feel the energy within you stabilizing, calming, and centering.

Hold your piece of blue agate or moonstone in your hands, closing your eyes, and taking several deep breaths. Allow the energy of the stone to calm your emotions and clear any emotional blockages.

Write down on the paper what you are feeling and why. Do not filter or judge, just let the words flow onto the page.

Now, place the paper in the bowl of water and let it soak. As it soaks, visualize the water absorbing all the negativity, hurt, anger, or sadness. Add a few drops of your chosen essential oil.

Once the paper is fully soaked, remove it from the bowl and let it dry. As it dries, visualize your emotional pain diminishing, just as the water evaporates from the paper.

Once the paper is dry, burn it using the flame of the candle, being careful to catch the ashes in a fire-safe container. As the paper burns, feel a sense of relief and emotional release.

Dispose of the ashes outside, returning them to nature.

Remember to express gratitude to the elements and to yourself for undertaking this journey towards emotional healing.

Meditation for Connecting with Water

This simple meditation helps you to deepen your connection with the element of water, encouraging emotional flow, intuition, and a sense of peace.

Steps:

Find a quiet place where you won't be disturbed. Sit comfortably, with your back straight. Close your eyes.

Begin by taking deep, calming breaths. With every inhalation, visualize yourself drawing in tranquility. With every exhalation, see yourself releasing tension.

Visualize yourself sitting on the bank of a peaceful river. Feel the moist, cool air on your skin. Hear the water gently flowing.

Now, visualize yourself stepping into the river. Feel the water against your skin. It's cool, refreshing, and calming.

As you stand in the river, imagine the water gently washing away all your worries, fears, and negative emotions. They're carried away downstream, leaving you feeling calm and emotionally balanced.

Stay in this state for as long as you wish. When you are ready, visualize yourself stepping out of the river, and the scene fading away.

Slowly bring your awareness back to your physical surroundings. Wiggle your fingers and toes, and when you feel ready, open your eyes.

Ritual for Enhancing Intuition

Water, being the realm of the subconscious and intuition, can be used to heighten your intuitive abilities.

Materials Needed:

A chalice or cup of moon-charged water

A piece of amethyst or lapis lazuli

Purple candle

Mugwort or lavender incense

Steps:

Create a sacred space. Light the candle and incense and place them on your altar. Hold the piece of amethyst or lapis lazuli in your hands, allowing its energy to attune you to the higher realms of consciousness.

Take the chalice or cup of moon-charged water in your hands. Close your eyes and attune to the water's energy. Visualize it glowing with a soft, silvery light, resonating with the energy of intuition.

Take a sip of the water. As you do, imagine the water's energy flowing through you, heightening your intuition and activating your third eye.

Spend a few moments in quiet meditation, allowing your intuition to guide your thoughts. Be open to any images, feelings, or insights that come to you.

Close the ritual by expressing your gratitude to the water and to your intuition for their guidance.

By incorporating these rituals and meditations into your practice, you can tap into the profound energy of water, enhancing emotional healing, intuition, and interpersonal relationships. In the next chapter, we will explore the importance of balance between all elements and delve into practices designed to maintain this elemental equilibrium.

Chapter 11: Elemental Balancing - Understanding the Need

Elemental balance is a cornerstone of elemental witchcraft and, indeed, of the entire universe. The Universe, our planet, and even our bodies are made up of the four elements—Earth, Air, Fire, and Water. When these elements are in equilibrium, we experience harmony and peace, both within ourselves and in our external lives. This chapter will delve into the importance of achieving this elemental balance and the potential implications if we fail to do so.

In all aspects of existence, balance is critical. Without it, systems tend to spiral into chaos or stagnation. Elemental balance is no different. Each element represents different aspects of our being. Earth corresponds to our physical body and practical affairs, Air to our thoughts and communication, Fire to our will and passion, and Water to our emotions and intuition. Imbalances in these elements can affect our physical, emotional, mental, and spiritual well-being.

Consider our bodies, a wonderful product of Earth. They are tangible, solid, and functional, like the element they resonate with. An excess of Earth energy could make us rigid, inflexible, and overly focused on material aspects. Conversely, a deficiency could make us feel unstable, ungrounded, and disconnected from reality. To maintain our physical health and stability in our lives, we need to ensure Earth is balanced within us.

Air, the element of intellect and communication, shapes our mental world. It is in our thoughts, ideas, and the ways we express them. If there's an excess of Air, we might find ourselves lost in thoughts, becoming overly analytical, or talking without taking action. On the other hand, a deficiency could lead to a lack of imagination, difficulty in expressing ourselves, or an inability to grasp complex ideas. A balanced Air element helps us think clearly, communicate effectively, and foster fruitful ideas.

Fire, the element of transformation and willpower, drives our desires, motivations, and courage. When Fire is balanced within us, we are passionate, determined, and enthusiastic. But an imbalance can distort these qualities. An excess could lead to aggression, impulsivity, and recklessness, while a deficiency might result in apathy, lack of motivation, and fear of change. Keeping Fire in check allows us to channel our passions rightly, take calculated risks, and embrace positive change.

Finally, Water, the element of emotions and intuition, governs our emotional responses and intuitive perceptions. When Water is in balance, we experience a healthy flow of emotions, and our intuition is sharp. However, an excess could lead us to become overly emotional, moody, or stuck in daydreaming, whereas a deficiency might make us emotionally closed, indifferent, and disconnected from our intuitive self. Maintaining the balance of Water ensures emotional equilibrium and a strong intuitive sense.

The necessity of elemental balance extends beyond individual well-being. It plays a crucial role in our interactions with others and our perception of the world around us. In relationships, a balanced Fire allows us to express love passionately yet respectfully, while balanced Water helps us understand and empathize with others' emotions. A balanced Earth keeps us committed and reliable, and balanced Air aids in clear and meaningful communication.

On a broader scale, our collective elemental balance influences societal dynamics. A society with balanced Fire is innovative and energetic, with balanced Earth it is stable and sustainable, with balanced Air it is intellectually thriving, and with balanced Water it is emotionally mature and intuitive.

As elemental witches, the task of maintaining this balance often falls to us. Understanding the elements within and ensuring their equilibrium is an integral part of our practice. It enables us to live holistically, align with the Universe's rhythm, and influence positive change.

But how do we know when we are out of balance? Elemental imbalances can manifest in many ways, from physical ailments to emotional turmoil, from a sense of aimlessness to a feeling of being overwhelmed.

In subsequent chapters, we will delve deeper into identifying these imbalances and provide practical rituals and meditations to restore the equilibrium.

Balancing elemental energies isn't merely about personal or societal wellness. It's about co-existing harmoniously with the world, aligning ourselves with the ebb and flow of nature, and thus playing our part in the universal symphony.

In the end, we are not separate from these elements; we are expressions of their intricate dance.

Recognizing this interconnectivity and working towards elemental balance is, therefore, not just necessary—it is fundamentally human.

The journey to elemental balance is ongoing, dynamic, and deeply transformative. As we navigate through life, learning, growing, and evolving, our elemental needs might shift.

Yet, the objective remains the same: to achieve a state of harmony where Earth grounds us, Air inspires us, Fire motivates us, and Water soothes us—a state where we embody the true essence of the Witch of the Elements.

Chapter 12: Elemental Balancing - Rituals and Practices

Finding harmony within yourself is akin to finding a beautiful melody amidst a cacophony of sounds. The elemental forces of Earth, Air, Fire, and Water within us often pull us in different directions, creating dissonance within our physical, mental, and emotional selves. Thus, it becomes essential to balance these forces, harnessing their unique properties to create an equilibrium within, allowing us to exist harmoniously with the universe.

This chapter is your practical guide to attaining this elemental balance. Herein, we will explore various rituals and meditations specifically designed to equilibrate the four elements, promoting inner harmony and alignment with the universe.

Ritual of the Elemental Balance

This ritual is best performed outdoors where you can be closer to the elements, though it can be adapted for indoor practice if needed.

Ingredients:

Four candles (colors representing each element – green for Earth, yellow for Air, red for Fire, and blue for Water)

A bowl of salt (for Earth)

Incense (for Air)

A lighter or matches (for Fire)

A bowl of water (for Water)

A pentacle (symbolizing Spirit)

Instructions:

Begin by setting up your elemental altar. Arrange the candles at cardinal points: North for Earth, East for Air, South for Fire, and West for Water. Place the corresponding elemental representations next to each candle. The pentacle, representing Spirit, is set in the center.

Light the incense and the candles in the order of Earth, Air, Fire, and Water.

Stand in front of the Earth candle. Sprinkle some salt into your hand, feel its texture, and say, "I call upon the element of Earth. Ground me with your stability and nurture me with your richness."

Move to the Air candle. Wave the incense smoke gently and say, "I call upon the element of Air. Enlighten me with your wisdom and inspire me with your movement."

Next, stand before the Fire candle. Feel the warmth of the flame and say, "I call upon the element of Fire. Ignite my passion and strengthen my will."

Finally, move to the Water candle. Dip your fingers in the water and say, "I call upon the element of Water. Nurture my emotions and enhance my intuition."

Stand in the center of your altar, placing your hands on the pentacle. Say, "I call upon Spirit, the element that binds all. Connect me to my higher self and the universe."

Close your eyes and visualize a balance of the elements within you. Feel yourself grounded by Earth, inspired by Air, energized by Fire, and soothed by Water. Let Spirit connect all elements within you.

When you're ready, open your eyes. Say, "Balance has been achieved. So mote it be."

Remember to extinguish the candles and clear the altar.

Elemental Balancing Meditation

This meditation is designed to maintain the balance achieved by the ritual and can be practiced regularly.

Sit comfortably and close your eyes. Breathe deeply, letting calmness wash over you.

Visualize a small seed in your core, representing Earth. Feel it grounding you, stabilizing your being.

Now, imagine a gentle breeze swirling within you, representing Air. It carries thoughts and ideas, clearing your mind.

Next, envision a small flame flickering inside, representing Fire. Feel it filling you with strength, passion, and determination.

Then, visualize a stream flowing within you, representing Water. It soothes and nurtures your emotions, promoting intuition.

Finally, imagine a bright light radiating from your heart center, embodying Spirit. Feel it connecting all elements, binding them together in harmony.

Sit with this balanced energy for a while. When you're ready, gently bring your awareness back to your surroundings. By incorporating these rituals and meditations into your practice, you can achieve a more harmonious existence, attuned to the elements and the universe. The journey to balance requires consistent effort and understanding, but with time, the melody of harmony will become your natural state of being. Embrace the elements, embrace yourself, and let the Witch of the Elements guide you towards balance and harmony.

Chapter 13: Seasons and Elements

One of the core principles of elemental witchcraft is understanding the interconnectedness of all things. The witch, the elements, the seasons—all these are intimately linked in a cycle of perpetual ebb and flow. In this chapter, we will explore the connection between the four seasons—Spring, Summer, Autumn, and Winter—and the elements. Understanding these relationships will allow you to align your practice with the natural cycle, enhancing the harmony between you and the world around you.

The dance of the seasons is a magical ballet choreographed by the Universe, each one associated with an element that reflects its essence. The birth of Spring is linked to Air, the heat of Summer resonates with Fire, the harvest of Autumn connects to Earth, and the stillness of Winter corresponds with Water.

Let's delve deeper into each season and discover the rituals, meditations, and practices that harness the elemental energies prevalent during these times.

Spring - The Breath of Air

Spring is the season of new beginnings. After the long, cold winter, life starts to stir again. Buds sprout on trees, flowers bloom, and animals come out of hibernation. This season is linked with the element of Air, representing intellect, communication, and fresh starts.

Spring is a perfect time to begin new projects or to breathe life into the ones that lay dormant during winter. Air-inspired rituals during this season might involve clearing out the old to make room for the new. Consider a 'spring cleaning' of your house, but extend this concept to your mind and spirit.

A simple Air meditation for spring could involve going outside on a windy day. Sit or stand where the wind can touch you. Close your eyes and feel the air rushing against your skin. Visualize this air clearing away the mental cobwebs and infusing you with fresh energy and new ideas.

Summer - The Passion of Fire

As spring gives way to summer, the world is in full bloom. The days are long, the sun is bright, and the heat is intense—this is the season of Fire. Fire represents transformation, passion, and willpower. The summer is a time to stoke the fires of your goals, to take action and drive your intentions into reality.

Fire rituals during the summer may involve bonfires or candle magic. A midsummer bonfire can be a powerful way to connect with the element of Fire. As you gaze into the flames, visualize your goals being transformed into reality. If a bonfire isn't practical, a candle ritual can serve a similar purpose. Light a candle that represents your intention, and as you watch the flame, imagine your desires being brought to light.

Autumn - The Stability of Earth

Autumn is the season of the harvest. It's a time to reap what has been sown, both literally and figuratively. As such, Autumn aligns with the element of Earth—representing stability, prosperity, and grounding.

In Autumn, it's time to give thanks for the physical and spiritual bounty you've received. Earth-based rituals during this season might involve creating an altar with symbols of your achievements or blessings. Meditating on these, feeling the weight of them in your hands, can help you to ground your accomplishments in reality and to feel gratitude for what you have.

Winter - The Intuition of Water

Winter, the final season of the year, is a time of introspection and rest. As the world around us slows down and becomes quiet, we are encouraged to turn inward. This inward focus aligns with the element of Water, representing emotions, intuition, and the subconscious.

Water rituals in the winter might involve meditative baths or reflecting by a body of water. A winter bath ritual, warmed with essential oils and salts, can be a powerful way to cleanse yourself of the year's energies and to prepare for the year ahead. If you have access to a body of water—a pond, a river, the ocean—spending time near it, even in the colder months, can help you to tap into your emotional and intuitive self.

Aligning your practice with the natural cycle of the seasons helps deepen your connection with the elements and the universe. As you observe the world around you, remember that you are not a separate entity, but a part of this beautiful, ever-changing tapestry. As you grow and change with the seasons, so do your elemental connections. By working with these energies instead of against them, you can live a more balanced and harmonious life.

Remember, the wheel of the year is not a rigid schedule but a guide. Each season holds all the elements within it to varying degrees. The element of the season simply has a louder voice, singing in harmony with the rhythm of the Earth. By aligning ourselves with this natural rhythm, we align ourselves with the universe, creating a life full of balance, harmony, and magical potential.

Chapter 14: Elements in Divination

Divination is an ancient practice that involves foretelling future events or seeking hidden knowledge through various forms of magical or mystical practices. In the realm of elemental witchcraft, divination takes on a whole new perspective as the elements themselves are used as a guide to the unseen world. By aligning with the energies of Earth, Air, Fire, and Water, a witch can invoke their particular qualities to bring about a deeper understanding and more meaningful divination experiences. In this chapter, we'll explore how the elements can be used in different forms of divination like Tarot, Runes, and Scrying.

Tarot and the Elements

Tarot is a rich divination system that comprises 78 cards divided into two parts: the Major Arcana (22 cards) and the Minor Arcana (56 cards). The Minor Arcana is further divided into four suits which correspond to the four elements: Cups (Water), Swords (Air), Wands (Fire), and Pentacles (Earth).

Earth - Pentacles: Pentacles are associated with the element of Earth, representing the material world, abundance, stability, and grounding. When Pentacles appear in a Tarot spread, they often signify issues concerning practical aspects of life such as work, money, or health.

Air - Swords: Swords symbolize the element of Air and represent thoughts, intellect, conflict, and action. A reading dominated by Swords often signifies mental struggles, decisions, and changes.

Fire - Wands: Wands are associated with the element of Fire, symbolizing inspiration, passion, willpower, and creativity. When Wands dominate a reading, it often indicates a period of growth, energy, and activity.

Water - Cups: Cups, connected to the element of Water, signify emotions, intuition, relationships, and healing. A spread rich in Cups usually points towards matters of the heart and emotional landscape.

Understanding the elemental associations within the Tarot can offer another layer of depth and nuance to your readings. The elements can help you understand the energy present in the situation and suggest potential approaches or resolutions.

Runes and the Elements

Like the Tarot, the ancient Runic alphabet is also deeply connected to the four elements. Each Rune not only carries a symbolic meaning but also relates to one of the elements. Although there are various ways to categorize Runes with elements, one common method includes:

Earth Runes: These Runes, such as Fehu, Wunjo, and Jera, often represent physical realities, practical matters, wealth, and prosperity.

Air Runes: Ansuz, Raidho, and Ehwaz, for example, can be associated with the element of Air. They symbolize communication, movement, and change.

Fire Runes: Fire runes like Sowilo, Thurisaz, and Kenaz represent transformation, action, and power.

Water Runes: Laguz, Gebo, and Ingwaz, which can be associated with the Water element, represent emotional matters, relationships, and life cycles.

As with Tarot, understanding the elemental associations in the Runes can enhance your divination practice by bringing an additional level of insight and context to your readings.

Scrying and the Elements

Scrying is another form of divination that involves gazing into a reflective surface to receive visions or messages. Different elements can be used as the medium for scrying.

Earth Scrying: This can involve gazing into crystals, stones, or even dirt. The stable and grounding nature of Earth can offer practical and realistic insights.

Air Scrying: This method involves using smoke or clouds as the medium for scrying. As Air is linked with intellect and communication, it can bring clarity to confusing situations.

Fire Scrying: This involves gazing into flames or embers. Fire's transformative and active nature can offer insights into potential changes and actions.

Water Scrying: The most common form of scrying involves water. It's often done by gazing into a bowl of water or a pond. As Water is associated with emotions and intuition, this method can reveal insights about emotional matters and subconscious thoughts.

The choice of element for scrying often depends on the question or issue at hand. By choosing the right element, you can align with its energy and draw on its unique qualities to gain deeper insights.

The elements form a vital part of many divination practices. By understanding their symbols within these systems and how to interpret them, you can enhance your divination skills and gain more precise and meaningful insights. But remember, divination is as much an art as it is a skill. It requires practice, intuition, and an open mind to interpret the messages that come through. Happy divining!

Chapter 15: The Fifth Element - Spirit

After exploring the traditional four elements and their place in witchcraft, we now turn to the element that binds them all together—the fifth element, Spirit, also known as Ether or Akasha in various traditions. The Spirit is what unites all elements, all beings, and all creation. It is the bridge between the physical and the spiritual, the tangible and the intangible. It is the divine spark within us and the limitless cosmic energy that pervades the universe.

Just as in physical nature, we have solid earth, flowing water, gusty air, and blazing fire, the quintessence of these elements—their life force, their spirit—emanates from Ether. It is the space that the other elements fill, the energy that they move within. Unlike the other four elements, Spirit doesn't have a specific direction or season associated with it. Instead, it is omnipresent, inherent in all directions and all seasons, linking all facets of existence together.

Embracing the Spirit element in our witchcraft practice helps us transcend the physical limitations of our human existence, allowing us to connect with the divine, the universe, and our higher selves. It brings balance and unity to our practice, harmonizing the energies of the other four elements within us. It is a symbol of our consciousness, our soul, our essence— the spiritual 'self' that persists beyond our physical form.

To incorporate Spirit into our practice, it is essential first to understand it— a task easier said than done. As Spirit exists beyond the physical realm, it can't be understood or explored in the same way we would with Earth, Air, Fire, or Water. We can't touch, taste, or see it. We can't contain it within a bowl or a jar. But we can feel it. We can sense its presence in the profound silence, in the quiet moments of deep meditation, in the undeniable interconnectedness of all life.

As witches, we often invoke the Spirit element when we cast our circles, acknowledging its presence and seeking its guidance and protection. It forms the center of our circle, the sacred space where we merge the energies of Earth, Air, Fire, and Water, and invoke the divine. The altar often represents this element in our ritual space, hosting the tools symbolizing the other elements.

Meditation is one of the most effective ways to connect with the Spirit element. It allows us to quiet our mind, shed our physical consciousness, and dive deep into the spiritual realm. Through regular meditation practice, we can enhance our perception of Spirit, understanding its subtle messages and its profound wisdom.

Try this simple Spirit meditation:

Find a quiet, comfortable space where you won't be disturbed.

Sit or lie down comfortably and close your eyes.

Begin by focusing on your breath. Feel the rise and fall of your chest, the air entering and leaving your lungs. If any thoughts arise, acknowledge them and gently bring your focus back to your breath.

Once you feel relaxed, visualize a brilliant white light in your heart center. This light represents the Spirit element within you—pure, divine, and boundless.

Gradually let this light expand, filling your entire body, making you feel light, serene, and connected.

Now visualize this light expanding beyond your body, merging with the energy of the universe. Feel your consciousness expanding with it, becoming one with the cosmos.

Stay in this state of unity and tranquility for as long as you feel comfortable.

When you're ready, gradually pull your consciousness back into your body, bringing the expanded light back into your heart center.

Take a few deep breaths and, when you feel ready, gently open your eyes.

Practice this meditation regularly, and over time, you'll notice an increased sense of interconnectedness, harmony, and spiritual awareness in your life. You'll feel more balanced and in tune with your practice, your environment, and yourself.

Aside from meditation, incorporating symbols of Spirit into your rituals can also help you connect with this element. This can be anything that represents the divine or the cosmos to you—a statue of a deity, a picture of the universe, a crystal ball, a pentacle, or even a simple white candle. Use these symbols in your rituals, on your altar, and in your sacred space to acknowledge the Spirit element and harness its energy.

In the next chapter, we'll explore more rituals and practices for working with the Spirit element, helping you integrate it more deeply into your witchcraft practice and your life.

Remember, the Spirit element is not an abstract concept to be understood intellectually but an experience to be felt profoundly. The more you open yourself up to this element, the more you'll connect with the limitless energy of the cosmos, finding balance, harmony, and unity in your magical practice and your life.

Chapter 16: Working with Spirit - Rituals and Practices

Often referred to as the fifth element, Spirit, also known as Ether or Akasha, stands apart from the other four elements. While Earth, Air, Fire, and Water relate primarily to the physical realm and our human experiences, Spirit is the bridge that connects us to the divine, the universe, and the realm beyond our immediate perception.

The Spirit element is often symbolized by the shape of a spiral or circle, indicating continuity, unity, and the infinite nature of existence. It represents our essence, our divine spark, and the magic that infuses all life. Working with Spirit encourages spiritual development, fosters connection with higher realms, and strengthens the bond between the physical and spiritual world.

Meditations to Connect with the Spirit

Meditation is a powerful tool for connecting with the Spirit element, inviting us to delve deeper into our subconscious mind and expand our awareness beyond the physical realm. Here are two meditations that can be practiced:

The Spiral Journey Meditation: This meditation helps in exploring the inner depths of your consciousness and connecting with your divine essence.

Start by finding a quiet, comfortable place where you won't be disturbed. Sit or lie down in a relaxed position and close your eyes. Visualize a spiral in front of you. See it as a pathway leading both inward and outward.

Inhale deeply, visualizing the breath drawing in the Spirit element, and as you exhale, see yourself moving along the spiral. As you journey along this path, be open to any insights or messages you may receive.

Keep your focus on the journey and not on the destination. You are exploring the infinite depths of your being and the universe. When you feel complete, visualize yourself stepping off the spiral and back into your physical environment. Slowly open your eyes and ground yourself.

The Starlight Meditation: This meditation connects you with the cosmos, reminding you of your universal connection.

In a comfortable position, close your eyes and imagine yourself standing under a starlit sky. Breathe in the cool, crisp night air, and as you do, feel a sense of tranquility washing over you.

Look up and see a bright star directly overhead. This star represents the Spirit element. As you focus on it, feel its energy descending like a beam of light, connecting with your being. Let this light fill you, connecting you with the vast cosmos and your higher self.

When you are ready, imagine the light retracting back into the star, leaving a sparkling thread, a connection that remains with you. Breathe deeply and open your eyes, carrying this cosmic connection with you into your everyday life.

Rituals for Working with Spirit

Rituals form an essential part of elemental witchcraft. They are powerful tools for harnessing and directing the energy of the elements towards specific intentions. Here are some Spirit-focused rituals:

Casting a Circle of Spirit: This is a variation of the traditional circle casting, invoking the Spirit element to create a sacred space.

To begin, clear and cleanse your space. Stand in the center of your space, holding your dominant hand or a tool, like a wand or athame, pointed upwards. Visualize a bright light above you, representing the Spirit element. Draw this light down, visualizing it creating a sphere around you.

As you do this, you may chant, "I invoke the Spirit, the divine essence, the bridge between realms. Surround me, infuse me, connect me. So mote it be." Feel the energy of the Spirit element around you, within you, and flowing through you.

Spirit Element Dedication Ritual: This ritual is meant to dedicate yourself to working with the Spirit element.

Create a simple altar representing the Spirit element. This could include a white or silver cloth, a chalice of clear water, a feather, incense, or any object that represents Spirit to you.

Begin by grounding and centering yourself. Light the incense or a candle and say, "I call upon the Spirit, the divine essence, the fifth element. Guide me in my journey, connect me with the higher realms, and infuse my magic."

Hold the chalice of water, representing the fluid nature of Spirit, and say, "With this water, I dedicate myself to the Spirit. May I be open to divine guidance and wisdom." Take a sip of the water, symbolically ingesting the Spirit element.

Working with the Spirit element is not just about performing rituals or meditations. It's about recognizing your divine connection, nurturing your spiritual development, and manifesting your magic. As the bridge between the physical and spiritual realm, the Spirit element reminds us that we are not merely physical beings having a spiritual experience, but spiritual beings having a human experience.

Engaging with the Spirit element encourages us to explore the infinite possibilities of existence, the mysteries of the universe, and our place within it. As we forge this spiritual connection, we find our magic, our power, and ultimately, ourselves. So mote it be.

Chapter 17: Conclusion - The Witch of the Elements

You have journeyed far into the heart of the elemental forces, breathing life into your witchcraft practice by forging a powerful bond with the Earth, Air, Fire, and Water. You've ventured deep within yourself and reflected your inner nature in the mirror of these primordial elements. You've discovered the unique weave of the elements within your own spirit, giving you insight and power to manipulate these forces for harmony, balance, and growth.

Elemental witchcraft is about understanding the core essences of life and harnessing them towards your intentions. From the grounding and nurturing Earth, the intellectual and communicative Air, the transformative and passionate Fire, to the emotional and intuitive Water, you've dipped your spirit into each of these elemental wells. You've also sought the fifth element, Spirit, the thread that binds these elements and us to the universe.

In the process, you've not merely learned spells, rituals, or meditations, you've truly become the witch of the elements, understanding the intricate tapestry of life and the universe. You've sought balance within yourself and the world around you, using the elements as your guide and tools.

But remember, becoming the witch of the elements is not a destination; it's a lifelong journey. Like the elements themselves, you must remain fluid and open to change. Just as each day brings a new sunrise, each moment brings a fresh opportunity to deepen your understanding and connection to these elemental forces.

The elemental balance you've worked to achieve isn't a one-time accomplishment—it's a dynamic equilibrium that requires continuous attention. Just as the earth needs the rain to quench its thirst, so too does the heart require love to remain tender. Balance is a harmony achieved through consistent efforts and adaptations. As you continue on your journey, your understanding of each element will grow and change, just as you will.

You've started to appreciate the elements in the world around you, observing their influence on the seasons and divination. Remember, they are always present and not confined to your rituals and practices. They permeate your existence, from the smallest grain of sand beneath your feet to the vast expanse of the sky above. They are in every gust of wind, every lick of flame, every ripple of water, and every fragment of earth. They are in every thought you think, every word you speak, and every emotion you feel.

As an elemental witch, your work does not stop with self-improvement and harmony. You've learned to harness the elements for personal growth and balance, but your reach extends further than your own being. You have the knowledge and power to create ripples of change and balance in the world around you. You can use your connection with the elements to nurture the Earth, to encourage intellectual conversation, to spark transformative change, and to enhance emotional understanding and intuition in your community.

From here, you can explore even further, branching into different aspects of elemental witchcraft. Perhaps you'll choose to delve deeper into the study of a particular element that calls to you or explore different ways to incorporate the elements into your existing practices, such as divination, shadow work, or other magical workings. Remember, your journey is unique, and there's no right or wrong path—only your path.

As you close this book, remember that you're not leaving elemental witchcraft behind; you're carrying it forward with you, rooted in your spirit. The elements are your partners, your guides, and your tools. They're part of your very existence and continue to shape and influence your path. Your relationship with them will continue to grow and evolve, just as the elements themselves are ever-changing.

You've kindled a flame of knowledge and power, sparked by the elemental forces. You are the Witch of the Elements, a being of balance and harmony, a child of Earth, Air, Fire, and Water, guided by Spirit. Your journey has been a testament to your strength, passion, and commitment to walking this sacred path. Carry this knowledge with pride and humility, remembering the responsibility it brings.

Your journey continues, filled with the promise of deeper understanding, richer connections, and magical experiences. As an elemental witch, you know the world is teeming with magic—it's in the rustling leaves, the dancing flames, the flowing rivers, and the fertile earth. It's in the words we speak, the love we share, and the dreams we chase.

You've come a long way, but remember, this is only the beginning. The world of elemental witchcraft is vast and deep, and there's always more to explore, more to learn, and more to experience. So here's to you, Witch of the Elements, may your journey be filled with magic, balance, and harmony. Blessed be.

Printed in Great Britain
by Amazon

39620265R00056